# Personal Branding: A Comprehensive Beginners Guide for 2020

By: Ben Smith

# Table of Contents

—

# Introduction

This book is designed to support you in identifying what it means to launch a personal brand, how to build one, and what it takes to leverage it.

In 2019, personal branding is one of the most powerful tools that you can use to support yourself in growing as a human, advancing in your career, and maximizing your earning potential. Although many do not realize it, we have been personally branding ourselves for generations as a way to increase our foothold in the professional world and advance to higher stages of our careers. With the introduction of the internet and the rise of entrepreneurship, however, personal branding has become more important than ever before. Whether you plan on leveraging your personal brand to help you advance in your corporate career or on using it to help you launch and sustain a successful company, personal branding is essential in the modern world.

Developing a strong personal brand can take time, practice, and consistency to really get it right. When you invest in your personal brand, you are truly learning how to embody a more professional and presentable part of yourself for your public persona to ensure that you are always leveraging your image. By doing this effectively, you can actually turn yourself into an asset for your clients or for any companies you might work for — making you more valuable and worth more to add to their team.

It is worth pointing out that even if you do not intend to, your online image and your public persona, in general, is always creating a reputation for you to live with. Whether you like it or not, this reputation will always follow you everywhere you go, which means that if you use it to your advantage, you can leverage it to help you advance in many areas of your life. Fortunately, it is not terribly challenging to brand yourself, either. In fact, you can easily begin branding yourself in an afternoon and then continue expanding off of that brand each and every day. As you continue developing your brand, you will find that it becomes easier for you to evolve it and create more traction with it over time — allowing you to *really* begin leveraging your personal brand for your own personal and professional growth.

If you are ready to get started with personal branding, let's dive in!

# Section 1: Branding Basics

# Chapter 1: Benefits and Opportunities for Personal Branding

Personal branding is one of the most powerful growth opportunities that we can harness in 2019 and beyond. When you brand yourself or cultivate your personal brand, you open yourself up to being able to take advantage of many key benefits and opportunities that are not often available to anyone who does not have a clarified and well-developed personal brand. In this chapter, we are going to explore the benefits and opportunities that you can gain from developing your personal brand so that you can see first-hand just how powerful this experience is.

## People Will Trust You

When you develop a brand for yourself, you create an opportunity for people to trust you because you put it all out on the table so to speak. Branding yourself is an excellent way to tell people why you are so passionate about what you do, what you are seeking to accomplish, and how you can support them. As a result, people are able to get a transparent look into who you are and they are able to begin developing a relationship with you through your reputation and image. In this day and age — thanks to digital marketing — even people who are not working directly with you or meeting you in person can get to know who you are and can develop a relationship with you through your brand image. As a result, you can actually have an incredibly massive impact of building trust with your audience through your personal brand online.

Developing trust is a powerful tool, as it supports people in feeling more naturally attracted to you. When it comes to leveraging your brand for profit, such as selling products or services or getting hired by a great company, you are more likely to be considered or accepted because you have already established trust with your audience. This trust can lead to higher sales or greater career opportunities because people already feel connected with you and trusting in who you are and what you have to offer.

# You Become an Asset

Being trustworthy, transparent, and visible can lead to you becoming a massive asset in your industry — whether you are working for a corporation or launching your own company. When people can trust you, clearly know your values and ethics, and can see you on a regular basis — they begin to see you as being an asset. This is the result of many things, ranging from you being "high in demand" to you being very visible and audible about what you have to offer for your industry. When you are visible, people can clearly see that you are good at what you do and that you are a great person to work with, which makes them more inclined to see you as being the best fit for fulfilling their unique needs.

The more people begin to recognize you as being a valuable asset, the more of an asset you become because you begin to have more and more people who want to work with you. As a result, people will be willing to pay more or offer you more lucrative opportunities to work together because they know that you are valuable. In other words, they compete for your time, and they are often willing to do whatever it takes to get your time because you are known for being great at what you do. As a result, you become a highly valuable asset to people's lives or businesses, so you get to do what you love doing and get much better pay and benefits for doing it.

## You Differentiate Yourself

If you are not open and visible in your personal branding, people will not have any clue as to why you are better than the next person who is doing exactly what you desire to be doing. Since you have not taken the time to differentiate yourself, you are not seen as being quite as valuable in the industry because no one really knows what you can do for them. In the age of the digital generation where everything can be discovered online and people can find out about the best "go to" person in any industry within seconds, it takes some effort to become that go to person. You need to establish your presence and increase your visibility so that people can see why you are so different from everyone else who claims to be doing what you are doing. This does not mean that other people may not do as great of a job as you can, but it does mean that you become more easily discovered when you are visible and available in the online world.

Differentiating yourself is valuable as it really begins to show people why you are the best at what you do and why you are the one that they need to be working with. When you are visible and sharing yourself and your talents online, you show people both why you are excellent at what you do and whether or not you are compatible with what they are looking for. As a result of human conditioning, and especially when it comes to business, most people do not want to waste their time developing relationships with people. Instead, they want other people developing relationships with them so that they do not have to put in quite so much effort. This may seem backward, but look at it this way: many people want the opportunities that you are aiming for which means just like you can become an asset, those opportunities are also assets. You need to be competitive by establishing yourself and creating relationships with people through your outreach to show why you are so different, highlight yourself as being compatible with your target audience, and increase the likelihood of *you* being the one who gets the opportunities.

## Authenticity Is Encouraged

With differentiating yourself being so important in the world of personal branding, it is natural that authenticity is not only admired but encouraged. Because you need to stand apart from others and get your name out there, it is important that you build your brand in an authentic manner that shows why you are so different from everyone else in your industry. In many cases, what differentiates us is not our values, our skills, or our image, but instead our actual personality. When you can infuse your brand with your authentic personality, you show people why they need to care and why they should care and you give them a reason to want to work with you. For this reason, authenticity is highly encouraged with personal branding.

The benefit of authenticity being encouraged is that you never have to feel as though you are putting on a mask to get the opportunities that you desire to have. Personal branding is not about becoming someone or something different so that you can increase your perceived value, it is about becoming more of yourself so that people can see your value more easily. As you become more of yourself, you build an entire career around being you which means that you never have to feel burdened or outshined by your business persona. Instead, you can be yourself and grow as an individual and allow your brand to grow alongside you. Furthermore, people expect you to be yourself which means that they are not continually pressuring you to become any different because they see you and your authentic personality as being so valuable.

## You Can Become a "Go-To" Expert

There are probably hundreds, thousands, or even hundreds of thousands of existing experts in the field that you are currently working in. As a result, if you are not working to brand yourself and set yourself apart from others, you are going to find yourself rapidly being consumed by the masses and hidden by your peers. You need to work on setting yourself apart and building your reputation in a positive manner so that you can not only become a more valuable asset in your industry but also so that you can become the go to person in your industry. To put it simply: people will think about the person they see and hear from the most, which will be you if your brand yourself effectively. They are more likely to remember the person that they have built a reputation with online and seen on a regular basis than they are to remember a person that they met once at a networking event and then never talked to again. You want to be the person they engage with regularly, not the person they rarely see, to ensure that you are the one that they think of when they think of your industry.

Becoming the go to expert in your field will take some time, consistency, and practice as people are going to need to see you around for a while in order to really get to know who you are. The more you get in front of your audience and talk about your industry, the more they will see you as the expert and continue looking toward you for advice. In no time, you will find yourself being the one they turn to as they begin to remember your name and your message and associate you with that subject in their life.

## You Can Attract More Aligned Opportunities

As you have already seen, being well branded means that you have the capacity to attract more opportunities your way as people begin to see you as a valuable asset to work with. When you attract these opportunities, perhaps one of the greatest things that you will realize is that these opportunities are far more aligned with you, your area of talent, and your ability to serve. You also position yourself in a place where you can negotiate your opportunities so that you can make them even more aligned, allowing you to experience greater opportunities and benefits from your personal brand.

People who are not leveraging their personal brand will always find themselves having to take whatever opportunities come their way because they do not have a high enough perceived value to be able to negotiate their deals. As well, they are not getting themselves recognized for their area of expertise so they are often not being presented with opportunities that are aligned with their needs and desires. When you choose to leverage your personal brand and make yourself known, it becomes a lot easier for you to get discovered by the right people and start being invited in for better opportunities. It is certainly worth it to brand yourself so that you can essentially tell people what you are looking for, show them that you are the right person for your ideal opportunity, and then begin receiving those opportunities.

## You Get to Choose Your Opportunities

In addition to being able to negotiate your opportunities, you also get to be pickier with the opportunities that you receive when you brand yourself. The more you brand yourself, the more perceived value you gain, and therefore the more power you have to decide what opportunities are aligned for you and which ones are not. As a result, you are going to be able to say no to any opportunity that does not directly align with what you are looking for and start taking on more of the ones that do.

In fact, when you brand yourself well enough that you begin to get this opportunity of choice over the opportunities that you take, you allow yourself space to increase your perceived value even higher. That is because, at this point, you are no longer just competitive in terms of who is trying to get your attention, but you are also competitive in terms of where you are willing to put your attention. This means that instead of you having to work so hard to make brands and companies see the value in you, they need to work harder to help you see the value in them so that you choose them over anyone else. Being in this position where you get to decide who and what opportunities you are willing to take up in your career is a powerful position to be in, and it awards you with many powerful opportunities that will bring about great change, too.

# Chapter 2: Who Can Create a Personal Brand? (Everyone!)

If you are wondering who personal branding is truly for, you will be excited to learn that personal branding is an ideal and excellent opportunity for everyone to take advantage of. The reality is this: every single person has a personal brand, whether they realize it or not. However, some people are not leveraging their built-in personal brand, so they end up not having the opportunity to take advantage of the many benefits that come in with leveraging it. If you do, then you are already far ahead of the rest of the crowd who still fails to see the value in branding yourself and leveraging your social image for personal and professional growth.

## What Is the Basis of a Personal Brand?

A personal brand is essentially your reputation—personified and enlarged. When you brand yourself, you take your outward persona, highlight all of your best qualities, and share them with others in a bold and recognizable way so that people can see you and engage with your brand. Everyone has a built-in personal brand, or a generalized reputation for themselves, which is why everyone can create a personal brand. The key is choosing to create a distinguishable personal brand that makes you stand out from the crowd while still keeping you authentic and true to yourself. When you learn how to leverage your personal brand without losing parts of who you are, suddenly, a world of opportunity and benefit opens up before you.

Since the basis of a personal brand is truly just your reputation, then everyone already has the basis of their brand built-in. All you need to do is identify what your reputation is, determine what you want your reputation to be, and then begin developing that reputation through all of your many ways of connecting with other people. For example, in conversations, on social media, and with your clients — you can spend time expressing your core values and beliefs and behaving in a way that is true to your desired personal brand or personal reputation. The more you do this, the more you lock in this reputation or brand and become known for who and what you are. As a result, you are personally branding!

# How Can One Leverage a Personal Brand?

You can leverage your personal brand in many ways, but the best way is to start by getting clear on what you want to be known for and then work toward determining how that can support you in achieving what you desire. For example, say you want to become the CEO of a major corporation — you would want to align your values with the values of the corporation and begin establishing your reputation as being a person who would be a perfect fit for that CEO position. The more you build a reputation or brand to position yourself for the results you desire, the more likely you will be able to generate those results.

There are countless different ways that you can leverage your personal brand, and oftentimes, the brand begins extending far beyond career opportunities as you begin to receive things like travel opportunities, the ability to network and create better relationships, and more. It starts with having a goal or a vision for yourself and then building a reputation that will enable you to fulfill that goal or vision. The more you learn how to effectively position yourself, the greater your chances will be at being able to create the opportunities that you desire.

---

## Will I Succeed?

Whether or not you will succeed is a question that only you can answer. When it comes to advancing and growing in life and in your career, you are the only person capable of looking at your unique situations and creating the opportunity for you to grow and succeed. If you are willing to do whatever it takes to succeed, including opening up your mind, working extremely hard and listening to what other people have to say and receiving feedback, then the chances of you succeeding are high. You must be willing to be considerate of your reputation and share your reputation openly and clearly when you are in positions where you can leverage your personal brand if you are going to grow and develop. Otherwise, you are not going to be able to effectively get your brand "out there" and make changes for yourself.

If you make the choice that you are ready to learn about what it means to personal brand and how you can create and leverage one and you are willing to put in the work to troubleshoot and grow, chances are you will do just that. The more you open yourself up to the willingness to grow, the more you will be able to leverage your personal brand to help bring in the benefits and opportunities that you desire. As you continue to grow, you will find yourself being exposed to many opportunities to not only create the results you intended to create but to also continue growing as a professional and as a person and setting your sights higher. In the end, if you are willing and committed, you can guarantee your growth. As for myself, I can guarantee that the steps outlined in this book are essential for you to create a solid foundation for yourself upon which you can grow from. If you follow these steps you will be well on your way to establishing and scaling a powerful personal brand.

# Section 2: Five-Step Strategy for Personal Branding

# Chapter 3: Discover Your Brand Identity

The first step in effectively cultivating a personal brand is discovering your brand identity. Since your personal brand is largely based around building a personal reputation in a scalable way, identifying your brand identity and narrowing it down is important. You need to be able to create a clear and distinct identity for your personal brand so that when it comes to scaling your brand and building your reputation, you know exactly what it is that you are scaling and building.

In this chapter, we are going to explore how you can begin identifying your brand in a clear and distinctive manner. You will discover what aspects of your brand need to be identified and clarified as well as which among them are fundamental to your overall growth as a personal brand. This way, you can start putting together a brand "personality" that you will go on to market as your personal brand.

# What A Personal Brand Identity Is Not, and What It Is

For starters, it is important that you understand what a brand identity is not. As we already discussed earlier, brand identity is not a mask that you wear that hides the real you from the rest of the world as you pretend to be someone that you are not. A brand identity is not meant to cause you to detach from parts of yourself or stop being the entirety of who you are so that you can cater exclusively to your career. In fact, any successful business person will quickly inform you that this is not the case and that you cannot focus exclusively on your career and your professional image if you want to achieve any level of success in your life. Learning how to build a brand that is authentic and not a false identity is imperative to ensuring that you are building it in a sustainable and healthy way.

When you are building your personal brand, your goal is not to try to *extinguish* parts of yourself but rather to *distinguish* parts of yourself. You want to focus on highlighting the parts of you that are most relevant to you being able to advance professionally when you are designing a personal brand so that you can amplify these parts in your branding. As you do, it is important that you choose to highlight things that are actually relevant to who you are and what you plan to offer in a professional front. Make sure that you are working with your passions and values and highlighting your unique characteristics so that people can easily identify your brand and your unique brand highlights, who you actually are and what you have to offer.

## Identifying What Matters to You

In order to begin building your personal brand identity, you need to start by deciding what your goal is or what your objective is with your personal brand. In other words, you need to identify what matters to you and what it is that you desire to create through your personal brand. This step is the very foundation upon which your entire brand will be built, so spend some time getting clear on what it is that you desire to create. As you begin to identify where it is that you want to be in life, learning how to position yourself to get there becomes a lot easier.

The first thing you should do is look at your bigger picture goal. Choose a period of time that you want to look forward to—whether it's a year away, five years away, ten years away, or fifty years away—and ask yourself what you want your life to look like. Consider both your professional and your personal life so that you can really get a feel for exactly what type of life it is that you desire to create for yourself. Of course, what you think right now and what you actually end up creating may be two entirely different things, but having a clear vision and focus is an important part of allowing yourself to grow forward and begin changing your experience. Ideally, you should write this vision down and get as clear as you possibly can with it.

Ask yourself questions like:

- How much money will I be making?
- What career will I have?
- Who will I be spending my time with?
- Where will I be living?
- What will my family situation be like?
- What lifestyle will I have?
- What will I be working toward?
- What will I be proud of accomplishing?
- What will matter most to me?
- What would an ideal typical day look like?

These types of questions help you clarify what matters to you so that you can begin building a vision and a foundation that actually serves what it is that you desire to create in your life.

---

Once you have this vision figured out, you need to start asking yourself what type of person you need to be in order to generate those results in your life. Knowing what type of person you would need to be as a person supports you in determining how you need to position yourself, what parts of your personality you need to highlight, and how you can begin moving toward having the career and lifestyle that you desire most.

After discovering what your vision is, you need to determine what your values and beliefs are. Your values and beliefs are key in helping you align with your dream and to position yourself in a way that is authentic and congruent to your thoughts and actions. Having clear values and beliefs allows you to convey a very specific message in your personal branding that will allow you to communicate directly to your target audience who, ideally, shares the same values and beliefs that you do.

When it comes to outlining your values, you want to pick just three or four core values that stand out for you in regards to who you are and what you care about, particularly in relation to the dream that you desire to create for yourself. It is important that the values you choose not only align with your desires and your target audience but also with you. Remember, the key here is to highlight who you are and amplify yourself in the industry, not create a false mask or a false persona that you think people are going to respond better to. While you do want to pick values that are relevant and that people care about, they also need to be relevant and important to you, personally.

## Discovering Your Differences

The next step, after identifying the base of your brand identity, is to start identifying what differentiates your personal brand from all of the other personal brands out there. Why are you the person that people need to work with over anyone else, and how can you build that into your image so that people can begin identifying you as being the go to person? How can you begin highlighting these qualities and sharing them in your brand so that you can really give people a feel for what it is that you are doing, why it is so important, and why you are the person who needs to be doing it?

The first way that you can identify your authenticity or your differences is by asking yourself what your superpowers are.

What are the things that you can do incredibly well, often better than anyone else around you? These should be the things that come naturally to you and that you excel in with little to no effort. Your superpowers are, essentially, your strengths and the things that you are incredibly talented with. You want to highlight your superpowers when it comes to developing your personal brand as this is your opportunity to show people what you are highly skilled in and how you can support them using your strengths. If your vision and values are your foundation, your superpowers are your sellable features, as these are the services or skills that you are going to sell to your audience. Even if you are seeking to grow your career and excel in a corporate structure, having these sellable strengths and skills sets you apart from anyone else who may be trying to grow into the same positions that you are.

In addition to your superpowers, you also need to consider your purpose. Your purpose is essentially your mission in life, or what means the most to you. Your purpose is typically limited to only one thing, and this one thing drives you and supports you in accelerating your vision to the next level. Generally, your purpose is the thing that wakes you up in the morning, motivates you to keep going even on challenging days, and inspires you to continue finding ways to overcome obstacles no matter how difficult those obstacles may be. When you know exactly what your purpose is, you can use it to both differentiate you and keep you motivated to continue growing even when it feels challenging or like there may be no way to proceed. Not only does it keep you moving forward, but your purpose will also differentiate you by giving you a different reason as to why you are working to create the results you desire and why it matters so much to you.

## Highlighting Your Personality

In addition to differentiating yourself, you also need to highlight your unique personality with your personal brand. Your personality is another aspect of who you are that will set you apart from everyone else in your industry as your personality is unique to you. Of course, you may have parts of your personality that do not necessarily cooperate well with your brand so learning how to choose the parts of your personality that serve your brand best is the ideal way to differentiate yourself without extinguishing your credibility. For example, if you are extremely playful and friendly but you are going for a more serious and focused career, toning down your playfulness so that you can amplify your seriousness in your professional life is important. As a result, you would likely want to focus on highlighting the more serious and focused aspects of your personality over your playful ones in your personal branding.

Aside from ensuring that the aspects of your personality that you are highlighting are on brand, allowing yourself the opportunity to really lean into your personality and express it clearly in your branding is important. You want to refrain from becoming another clone of the people that already exist in the online space to avoid having yourself being seen as "just another person in (your industry.)" What really sets people apart is their personality and how they express themselves uniquely in the industry, as this makes them memorable. You already have the foundation and the sellable features, so your personality is how you ensure that people think of you when they are looking to buy what you have to offer.

Think of it this way: if you go to a networking event and you see twelve guys in suits, who are you most likely to remember? The ten who sat around using similar vocabulary and carrying themselves in a similar way as they behaved just like the other nine guys, or the two who showed their personalities? Likely, you will remember the two who showed their personalities because they opened up enough to make themselves memorable and they also set themselves apart from the others. Not to mention, when people feel comfortable opening up with their personalities they often also feel comfortable creating relationships with people, which means that they are more likely to actually approach you and create meaningful conversation. As a result, you end up remembering these people more because not only do they have a strong foundation and similar values to you, but they also have unique skills and strengths and an authentic personality.

When it comes to branding yourself, being the person who not only differentiates themselves through what they have to offer but also through how they show up is important. This type of branding is going to allow you to really deepen your relationships with the people who follow you and maximize your ability to tap into these connections for further growth and benefits later on. It is important that you leverage your personality as a way to create a human face for your brand and a persona that people can relate to so they truly connect with you and think of you first when your industry comes to mind.

## Putting It All Together

Once you have highlighted your foundation, sellable features, and personality, it is important that you put it all together! Putting it all together allows you to combine three powerful layers of your brand into one thing to create the "behind the scenes" image of who your brand is and what you are all about. This is a simple process to do, you can literally visualize your foundation, differentiators, and personality coming together in three separate layers and creating one identity that becomes your brand. In the next chapter, we will personify this brand so that it truly resembles a *personal* brand and not just a business — but in the meantime, you need to put together the business end of your brand. Through doing this, you create a deeper brand that has a greater purpose for the people who follow you.

Here is an example of what the layers together might look like based on other companies and brands who are already doing this:

- Tony Robbins is a motivational speaker whose vision is to change the world and live a luxurious lifestyle while teaching others to do the same through mindset. He does this through his strengths of motivational speaking and understanding the human psyche. He stands out with his masculine personality that explains everything in very practical and logical ways while also staying motivational and inspirational. He is also known for having a sense of humor, a sincere side, and a tendency to be very vulnerable to his audience.
- Nike is an athletic company whose vision is to help everyone get fit and stay active in their lives in the way that suits them best. Their strength is creating a variety of fitness products that can support people with all different levels of athleticism and passion and in all different sports so that people in every area of the sporting world have high quality tools to use during their sports. Nike's personality is all inclusive, inspiring, motivational, and humble.
- Amanda Frances is a money mindset and business coach who has a vision of helping women create financial wealth for themselves through businesses that they love. Her strengths are communication, storytelling, and sharing things in practical and inspirational ways so that people can grasp the concepts behind the messages that she shares. Amanda's personality is very friendly, classy, upbeat, and inspirational. She also enjoys sharing practical facts, highlights of her luxurious life, and her passion for letting things be easy and comfortable with her audience.

Every brand has layers that create depth for who they are, what they have to offer, and how they can support people in growth. When you tap into these layers and allow yourself to awaken to the depth of yourself, creating your personal brand and adding enough layers into it to personify your brand and make it memorable and relatable is easy. You should practice putting your three layers together in a short bio like the ones explained above so that you can get a clear and concise visual of what it is that you want to create and put out there and how you can stay on-brand at all times. This will also make it easier for you to add texture to your brand through your personification practices that you will learn in Chapter 4.

# Chapter 4: Personify Your Brand

As a personal brand, a powerful tool that you can tap into is personifying your brand so that you can begin to create not only an identity for your brand but an actual personality that people can interact with and begin to build a relationship with. Personifying your brand turns it into a consistent "character" or entity that people can engage with and enjoy coming into contact with on a regular basis. When you personify your brand, you ensure that people are able to really identify who and what you are all about through this personification.

Personification is often done through generating a tone, a specific vocabulary, and an image. You also want your brand to be identified as being a part of a certain descriptive category — such as empowering, humorous, loyal, devoted, or motivating. These different elements of your brand's personification take your brand from being just an identity to becoming an actual entity, and it helps people connect with your brand on a deeper level. When it comes to personifying your personal brand, the key here is not only about how people perceive your brand but also about how you behave in association with your brand when it comes to other people. By having a clear brand personality in place, you know exactly how you need to be interacting with other people in order to create consistency in your brand. Truly, you are giving yourself permission to behave in ways that are authentic to you and that support you in having positive conversations and relationships with people so that you can promote your brand's reputation.

In this chapter, you are going to learn how to take your brand identity and personify it so that you can begin having regular and consistent engagements with your audience in a way that allows your brand to be amplified with your audience. It is important that as you start learning how to personify your brand, you choose to do it in a way that is authentic and relevant to who you are as a person. Again, because you are launching a personal brand, you want everything to feel very authentic and real to you, including the actual persona or personality that you are putting out there for everyone to see and experience. Make sure that you stay aligned with who you truly are.

# Overall Brand Visual

The first thing you need to do is look at your overall brand visual and start getting a sense for how your brand visual is coming across in all ways. You want to get an idea for what people are going to be looking at, how they are going to be perceiving you, and what you want them to notice most about you and your brand. A great way to get into this is to begin by considering your brand as being an actual person other than yourself and asking yourself what it is that you would want to see or perceive within your brand. Ask yourself – if you were to be the one giving you opportunities or purchasing from yourself, what about your personality and image would be the thing to stand out most to you? How would you want your brand to engage with you, communicate with you, and share with you?

If you have challenges doing this, consider taking an image of someone from the internet and turning that person into your brand. Point out what they look like, what they sound like, what they say, how they build relationships, and how they build themselves. Get really clear on what it is that sets them apart, how they identify to the people around them, and what about them makes them so interesting and enjoyable to follow and pay attention to. Highlight the reasons why everyone likes this person and wants to do business with them as well as what about them really leaves that positive and lasting impression on others. The more you do this, the better your understanding of your personal brand gets, which makes it easier for you to create your brand personification features with mindfulness for what your audience will see, perceive, and experience from your brand.

## Your Image

The first thing you want to get really clear with when it comes to personifying your brand is your brand's image, which is the first thing people are going to see when people look at you or your branding online. Your image is really your opportunity to take people's first impressions and turn them into a positive reflection of who you are and what your brand is all about. While in many cases, we would like to believe that looks do not matter — when it comes to personal branding, looks *are* very important. You need to be building an image that shows that you care about how people perceive you, that you are mindful of how your image and behaviors influence other people's thoughts about you, and that you are creating an image that clearly aligns with your values.

Your image is going to be defined by two categories — what you actually look like and how you carry yourself. You want to create a look that is going to be easy for people to identify and recognize as being yours so that people can easily spot you through your imagery and visual branding aids. In addition to helping keep your image consistent, proper visual branding will also help people think about you more even when you or your brand are not present. For example, if you brand yourself with gold type font often, when your loyal followers see gold type font elsewhere they will naturally begin thinking about your brand. If they have not engaged with your brand in a while, they may even grow curious about you and check back in to see what you have been up to, helping them turn their eyes back to you and your brand. Proper visual branding in this way creates a powerful opportunity for you to establish brand recognition with people, which results in your audience being able to easily and effortlessly associate your branding or elements of your branding with you.

In addition to the static visual images that you are sharing with people, you also need to consider the moving image of who you are—or the image of how you carry yourself in front of your target audience. How you carry yourself is valuable as you begin to see yourself as being the personification of your brand in action and allowing other people to see that as well. If your actions and physical movements and image does not align with your brand, people are going to think that your brand is false or not strong and they are going to avoid doing business with you. For example, if you create a brand that shows you as being professional and poised but you carry yourself with a lack of confidence and an unwillingness to learn how to effectively communicate with others, people are going to pick up on this disconnect. Likewise, if you brand yourself as being playful and fun but you always come across as being exceptionally shy or serious in the flesh, people are going to think that you are not as playful or fun as you claim to be. As a result, they will begin to see you as a brand that is showing up claiming to be something they're not which can greatly diminish your credibility and cause people to stop paying attention. For this reason, you need to create an image that honors how you actually show up and what mannerisms you naturally have to ensure that your moving image and static image are aligned.

Our moving images, or our mannerisms and the way that we

carry ourselves are unique from our static image in that we can actually evolve these images, so if you find that there are certain aspects of yourself or your brand that you want to amplify you can always focus on growing these skills. That being said, make sure that you do not begin prematurely marketing yourself as this person until you are confident in the skills that you have created. The more you begin to build your intrapersonal skills and organically sharing those as a part of your branding, the more your brand will evolve and the easier it will be for you to show your improvements off to potential clients or employers. So, to summarize, the moving part of your brand image will evolve regularly, but the static image of your brand needs to evolve slowly to avoid confusing people and severing your opportunity to establish brand recognition.

## Your Tone

The tone of your brand is how you come across when you are sharing information or connections with people who are interested in engaging with your brand. Your tone refers to the energy or emotion that is being expressed in your language and in your messages that you are wanting other people to pick up on. In order to identify what your brand tone needs to be, you will need to ask yourself what tone fits and serves best in your industry so that people can relate to you and begin to see you as being the person with that particular emotional layer. For example, if you are in the finance industry you may find that you serve best and are best perceived by others when you carry your emotional tone as being confident, educated, and communicative. If you are a life coach, you may find that you serve best and are perceived best by others when you carry your emotional tone as being inspirational, compassionate, and supportive. You need to learn which tones are going to convey the proper message to your audience while also helping you create an overall image that your brand can become best known for.

You can develop your tone by looking around at your idols in your industry and getting a sense for what their tone is, and for how it works. Pay attention to tones that seem to remain consistent through all of your idols, as these tones are ones that are likely necessary in your industry in order to be able to truly and effectively connect with your audience. In addition to highlighting these core tones within yourself, make sure that you also highlight the core tones that set you apart and make you unique from everyone else. For example, if you were to look at your idols you would likely notice that in addition to having common or similar tones they also have aspects of their tone or emotional representation that differs from others in the industry. They may not be so different that no one else is doing it, but they may be more different in the sense that they do not look and sound exactly like everyone else in your industry. Instead, they sound different. As a result, they stand out more and gain more traction in building their presence and becoming recognized by those around them, such as yourself.

## Your Vocabulary

In addition to how you say things, you also need to consider what exactly it is that you are saying in your conversations and in your social sharing updates. When it comes to what you say, it is important that you speak with a language that is relevant to what your audience actually pays attention to and understands. If you use words that are not common to your industry and that do not resonate with your audience, people are going to ignore you because you are not speaking in a way that is relevant to what your audience is looking for. Ideally, you should naturally have a familiarity with how the language in your industry sounds as you have likely been an observer of it, or even actively engaged in it, for some time now. By having a familiarity, it becomes easier for you to speak the same language as your audience does in a way that helps them actually resonate with you and connect to the words that you are sharing with them.

As an observer, the way that you speak in your industry is slightly less important because you are not actually trying to create a brand for yourself and leverage that brand for your personal opportunities. When you become a personal brand, you need to become more strategic about how you connect with your audience by being more intentional about what you say. If you have ever heard of "keywords" then you know how important your vocabulary is when you are branding yourself as a business or as a professional. These keywords are essentially hot words or words that are popular and frequently used in your industry when people are talking about matters relating to your industry. If you desire to create traction, you will need to identify these keywords and learn how to introduce them into your own vocabulary in a meaningful and powerful manner. Ideally, you should begin paying attention to what your own audience is saying and then practice sharing your messages through the same

---

language that your audience is sharing in order to be well-received. This way, you are getting your message across in a way that actually makes sense to the people you are talking with.

Language has a tendency to shift and change over time, especially as new concepts and pieces of information are introduced to your industry over time. For that reason, you should always be paying attention to the language that people are using and focusing on bringing that language into your own vocabulary so that you can stay relevant and interesting. If you see new words or trends arising in the vocabulary of your industry, instead of avoiding it or attempting to push it away, embrace those new words and learn how to use them. People will appreciate seeing you flow with the changing times and you will have an easier time staying connected with your existing audience and connecting with new members of your audience through this very behavior.

## Your Relationships

The way that you create relationships with people through your brand is important, as people want to develop relationships with you and they are going to want to experience consistency in the relationship building process. If you take the time to create an idea for how you want to build relationships in your brand and what you want those relationships to look like, it allows you to create a foundation for how you will build these relationships and how you will contribute in them. As a result, your audience comes to know you as a very specific person and has a clear distinction of who you are and who you are in relation to them.

Knowing how you want to establish relationships with people is crucial as it enables you to establish relationships in a meaningful and powerful way. Furthermore, the way that you establish relationships not only personifies your brand but also helps you create a very distinctive element of your brand that people can come to know and appreciate. For example, say you are a financial advisor. You could build relationships as being people's financial teacher and you could establish the relationship of being the person that people come to when they are looking for education on finances because they trust that you will be their teacher and teach them. Or, in a completely different branding method, you could become their friend who they seek for guidance and support in making their own decisions. In one relationship people see

---

you as knowing everything they need to know so they can rely on you to tell them what decisions are the right decisions are for them, in the other people see you as being an empowering guide so they can rely on you to empower them to make your own decisions.

When it comes to building relationships in your brand, there is no right or wrong methodology as long as you are staying professional, friendly, and focused on serving in your relationships. Aside from that, how you make relationships will need to be an organic process that feels right for you and the specific audience that you are targeting. If you are not entirely sure as to what your audience wants or needs from you, consider creating relationships that feel right for you and then paying attention to what those early relationships look like for you and what role you are needing to play in them. If you like the clients you have been working with and you want to continue working with them, you will want to take that role and leverage it to become the foundation for how you develop relationships with people so that you can play that role for others. As a result, you will find yourself establishing a clear and consistent element of your brand based on how you relate to others, which will directly impact your reputation and the development of your brand.

# Yourself

Lastly, you need to consider yourself and how your relationship with yourself is portrayed in your branding as well. Since you are branding yourself, people are going to want to see how you focus on personal development, how you relate to yourself, what you think about yourself, and how you behave as an individual, too. This means that you are going to have to pay attention to how your relationship with yourself fits in with your brand and how you can use it to not only make yourself seem like a true person and not just a static brand but also to establish credibility. For example, if you are a business coach that regularly talks about the importance of researching your industry but you do not show yourself ever researching your industry, people may think that you do not practice what you preach. So, by showing that you are doing the things that you claim others need to be doing, you show that you are not only a brand but an embodiment of your brand that can truly support others through personal hands-on knowledge of how to grow and succeed.

This means that if you are not already doing what you tell others to do, or if you are not embodying what someone in the successful position that you desire to be in would do, you need to start. Focus on developing your habits, creating a more powerful mindset, and approaching your personal and professional life in the way that someone with the success that you desire would. As a result, you will begin to actually embody it and people will see you as being more credible and reliable because you are exhibiting that you not only know the knowledge but you use the knowledge. When people begin to realize that you are using the knowledge and succeeding with the results that you claim you can create, they will start paying attention and within no time at all the traction you need to grow will escalate and you will find yourself rapidly evolving.

# Chapter 5: Practical Steps to Developing Your Brand

Now that you have the foundation and personality of your brand designed, you need to start creating the practical elements of your personal brand! This practical brand development is important for allowing you to begin creating a brand that will actually succeed in being seen and followed by the people who you are interested in targeting. Practical brand development includes doing things like creating a slogan, developing an online presence, and creating value or content for your audience to begin indulging in so that they can see how powerful you are and what type of information you have to offer.

In this chapter, you are going to learn about which practical steps are right for you, how you can be taking them in your brand development, and how they will help transform your brand. This piece of the puzzle can be summarized as being your "connector" or the way that you connect your brand to your audience so that they can discover you and realize that you actually exist. As a result, they will be able to continue

---

following you and engaging with your brand and developing strong relationships with you so that when you make offers or make yourself available for opportunities they are available to show up and meet you with them. Some branding or business coaches call this part "doing the work" because this is the part of personal branding where it becomes your job to not only be a brand but to get your brand out there so that people can find you. As long as you commit to doing the work and you do it in a way that is relevant to your brand, you will discover that growing your brand is not nearly as challenging as you might have thought it would be.

## Pick Your Slogan

Every brand is known for something, and often that something is their slogan. Nike has "Just do it;" McDonald's has "I'm lovin' it;" Subway has "Eat fresh." Every brand and even personal brands have slogans that they use on a consistent basis that they eventually become well-known for having. As a personal brand, having a slogan allows you to summarize your objective or your focus in a few words while also developing brand recognition. When you consistently say and use your slogan, people begin to associate you with your slogan because they remember hearing you say it all the time. As a result, even if they hear someone else say your slogan they begin to think of you and your brand, which helps them feel like they have an even deeper relationship with you. This deeper relationship also means that any time your audience wants something that you have to offer, you will be the first person that they think of because you are their connection, so you are more likely to get their business. Through this, all of those great opportunities that we talked about in Chapter 2 begin to open up for you so that you can really begin leveraging the value of your personal brand.

Creating a slogan can be somewhat intimidating, particularly if you are considering the fact that your slogan will need to remain the same for a long period of time. That being said, you can always allow your slogan to evolve with you slowly and over time if you need to until you land on the right one. For example, Pepsi has had more than 30 slogans before it landed on "Something for everyone." Sometimes, taking the pressure off of trying to decide what your slogan is going to be long-term and instead deciding on what it should be right now is important.

Once you have taken the pressure off, you simply need to

choose a slogan that is short, catchy, and descriptive of what it is that you are creating or that you desire to be known for.

You will want to choose one that is going to be flexible as well so that you can share it in multiple situations, allowing you to gain many opportunities to actually share your slogan and be seen using it. If you are feeling uninspired or uncertain, here are some examples of things to consider to help you create your slogan: you can stake your claim, make a metaphor, adopt your customer's attitude, create a rhyme or a play on words, or literally describe what you have to offer.

Some examples of great slogans, aside from those listed above, include:

- Death Wish Coffee: "The world's strongest coffee"
- Cards Against Humanity: "A party game for horrible people."
- Folgers Coffee: "The best part of waking up is Folgers in your cup."
- Aritzia: "Women's fashion boutique."

Choosing something simple, memorable, and useable is a great opportunity to create a slogan that you can use often and in many ways. Then, once you have made your slogan, you will want to use that slogan in as many areas of your brand as is naturally possible to ensure that you are creating memorability with your slogan. This way, when people think of you and your brand they automatically think of your slogan, which can make thinking about your brand fun. As well, if you combine your slogan and your imagery, you might also find that people associate various symbols with your brand that also inspires them to think about your slogan. For example, these days when people see a check mark they will often think of Nike and "Just do it" even if they are not actually looking at a Nike branded item. As a result, Nike is highly memorable, engaging with their audience even outside of their own efforts, and generating traction and success in their business.

## Define Your Message and Purpose

Part of creating your brand in a practical sense is taking the identity and persona of your brand and turning it into an actual message. Brands often have vision statements or mission statements that help convey what they are trying to create with their brand. This message or vision statement clearly tells people what they value, what they are focused on, and how they intend to make an impact on their brand. Oftentimes, brands will have a single statement as well as a complete message that they want to convey—and in many cases, you can easily find this information on their website or simply by asking them about it.

When it comes to personal branding, creating both a mission statement and a message is a valuable way of clarifying what it is that you are doing in messages that you can share directly with your audience. If you have a website, you can always share this information on your website so that people can easily see it and get a feel for what it is that you are creating in the world. If you do not, you can always just keep these written down on a piece of paper for you to read and pay attention to so that any time you are looking to create something or do something with your brand you can refer back to your mission statement and support others with it. Keeping these mission statements and messages available can be extremely powerful when it comes to branding and scaling so do not overlook this step, even if you think you already have a general idea of what it is that you are creating.

Your mission statement should be around one to two sentences long and should encompass a very direct and specific message in regards to what it is that you are wanting to accomplish through your work. Your mission statement is different from your slogan because it has more information in it and it is presented in a more formal and professional manner, as opposed to your slogan which is used as more of a branding or marketing tool than anything else. So, make sure that your mission statement is more practical and complete in regards to sharing what it is that you are all about and what it is that you are seeking to accomplish through your personal brand.

Your message should be what change that your brand — or you — aspires to create in the world. This can be a more elaborated version of your mission statement and it should include information such as why you are passionate about creating the impact that you desire to create and how you intend to create it. You can talk about what inspired you to begin, what causes you to stay so dedicated to your cause, and what you are doing to ensure that no matter what happens you will achieve your goal. By creating this more sentimental story with your reason, purpose, and desires, it becomes easier for you to share with your audience why you are so passionate about creating the impact that you desire to have. As a result, people see not only what it is that you are attempting to accomplish but why, and why it is so important to you to make sure that you do accomplish it. This added layer of intimacy through your brand helps people feel even more connected to you, which results in them staying dedicated to your brand and following your story.

## Design A Brand Board

Brand boards, or mood boards as many graphic designers call them, are a powerful tool to put together the visual image of who you desire to be as a brand and how you desire to portray your brand to your audience. When you use a brand board, you create your brand image in a more official manner as you go from conceptualizing a brand image to actually creating one that you can use in all of your marketing materials. In the past, creating a brand board for a personal brand may not have been quite so important as sharing was mostly done through word of mouth and networking. These days, however, social media provides us with an excellent opportunity to build a brand where each thing we share has a certain degree of longevity and also connects together with everything else we are sharing to create an overall image. Creating an image that makes sense, that flows nicely, and that draws people in is a powerful opportunity to leverage the longevity of the internet to build an intricate brand that helps you create even more opportunities for yourself in the professional world.

As you create your brand board, there are four primary elements that you will want to incorporate to help you generate a powerful visual for you to use. First, you want to decide what colors you are going to use for your brand when it comes to designing visual aids such as graphics, text colors, and website palettes. Ideally, you should have 1-2 main colors, 1-2 secondary colors, and 1-2 highlight colors. Having a healthy amount of colors incorporated into your brand allows you to create a wide range of graphics that will generate a greater visual appeal through your visual branding. Make sure that you capture not only the colors themselves but also the HTML and RGB codes so that you can input your chosen brand colors into your website, graphic design applications, and other online databases where you may need to use your brand colors.

Once you have your brand colors, you will want to choose a series of images that represent how you want those colors to come together and the mood for how you want your brand to be portrayed. This is why it is often called a "mood board," because you will be summarizing the tone of your brand in a few images that create the overall aesthetic and mood that you desire your brand to have. So, if you want a fresh and natural health brand you might consider using images of plants, white surfaces, and other clean and fresh looking items and spaces to generate the image and feel of something that is healthy and natural. If you are creating a fun and playful brand, you might incorporate many colors and choose images that show people having fun doing things like eating ice cream, dancing and listening to music, or riding bicycles. Choose the images that give you the feel that you want to give to others and generate your mood board from those images.

Next, you want to choose what fonts are going to be associated with your brand. It is important that you choose fonts that are going to be compatible with your overall image so that they help tie together the look that you have going. Make sure that your fonts also have the same mood or energy that you want your brand to have to make sure that everything flows together. For example, if you have a playful and fun brand you might choose fonts like Comic Sans, whereas if you have a more professional brand you might choose fonts like Helvetica. You will want to pick 1-3 varieties of fonts so that you can create headers, sub headers, and body text using your font profile. Some brands do choose to keep it simple and will use only one font and simply change the size and weight of the font for each different need to ensure that they stand out while also still creating a uniform profile. You can choose to create your font profile however you want to, as long as it feels like it fits the image of your brand.

Lastly, you are going to want to create a logo. Not everyone has a logo for their personal brand, but if you want to be professional and grow larger you are going to need to have a logo to support you in having a uniform brand image. If you are not familiar with how to create logos yourself, you can always hire someone to create the logo for you so that you can begin using that logo on all of your graphics and in your emails and other marketing campaign locations to ensure that you are building brand recognition. Again, make sure that the logo incorporates your font profiles, that it matches your brand image, and that it fits in with your overall brand mood. Keeping your brand organized this way will ensure that it looks professional and that you are building a consistent image so that you can start leveraging brand recognition for yourself.

## Create Your Foundation

Creating a foundation for your brand means determining how

you are going to get your brand out there. This is an important step so that you can begin sharing your brand with the people who would be the most likely to have a desire to do business with you. You will need to decide where you are going to focus your efforts to ensure that you are having maximum success connecting with your target audience and generating the results that you desire. Right now, your focus should be less on how you are going to build these platforms and more on how these platforms are going to support you in achieving the goals that you desire in your professional industry.

When it comes to growing a personal brand, there are many different platforms that you can consider leveraging to help you get your name out there and begin creating success with your brand. Depending on what type of brand you run, you will want to decide whether you want to run your brand partially online and partially offline, or exclusively online. It is not recommended to run your personal brand exclusively offline in the modern world as the internet allows for far greater reach and more consistent visibility so that people can find and interact with your brand on a regular basis. Although you can certainly have offline elements of your brand, staying exclusively offline can really hold you back from being able to generate any degree of success in your personal brand.

As you start to proof platforms for you to use when it comes to building your personal brand, it is important that you consider your objective and what it is that you are trying to create with your brand. Go back to your goals from earlier in this book and consider how you can achieve those goals through various platforms, then align yourself with the platforms that are going to help you achieve those goals. Researching your platforms properly now will ensure that when you start building into your platforms you are building on ones that are actually going to support you in aligning with your goals and getting there as quickly as possible. For that reason, you want to be very clear in how you are going to use them, how they are going to serve you, and what you are going to look to gain from them so that you can tell whether or not they are working. This way, you can be very clear in how your platforms are working for you and what you might need to do to adjust your approach to ensure that you are getting the most out of your efforts.

When you are researching online platforms, make sure that you start by paying attention to what the typical demographic for each platform is so that you can determine whether or not that demographic lines up with who your brand will be targeting. Spending time on the platforms where your target audience spends time is the best way to make sure that you are getting in front of them quickly and building a brand reputation for yourself quickly, too. The more you post and share in front of your target audience, the more they will see you and the better your chances at becoming recognized. As a result, you will start getting more opportunities even quicker.

It is also a good idea to pay attention to the way that the platform works to see if you are going to be able to actually leverage your chosen platforms to get in front of your audience. Consider what type of content it is that you want to be sharing with your audience and make sure that you are using a platform that nurtures that particular type of content so that you can really provide a lot of value to your target audience. There are several major social media platforms out there that you can use to help you get in front of your audience, so scan through them and see which ones you are going to be able to leverage the most.

Chances are, you are already on social media in a personal capacity so it is important that you make sure that you avoid using your existing opinion to influence your decision for what platform you are going to be spending most of your time on. You do not want to avoid using the proper platform for your brand because in a personal capacity you do not enjoy using it. Remember: this is about getting in front of your target audience and making a name for yourself, approach your brand and your brand strategies like a business to avoid letting your personal judgment influence your choice and take away from your success.

When it comes to offline platforms, you also need to spend time considering where you are going to get the best opportunity to get in front of your target audience and start growing your brand. For example, if you are growing a business where you want to be doing speaking engagements, make sure that all of the speaking engagements you are involved with are going to be ones where your target audience will actually be present. Getting in front of the right audience to speak, joining the right networking events to meet the right people, and advertising in the right areas are all necessary to make sure that you are not wasting your time and effort in places where you are not going to meet the people that you need to meet.

As you browse through platforms, it may become

overwhelming if you find that many of these platforms seem as though they could support you in reaching your target audience and generating success. In that case, you are going to want to narrow it down to 2-3 online platforms and 2-3 in person platforms to avoid being overwhelmed. Trying to get yourself in front of too many audiences at once will result in you stretching yourself thin and overwhelming yourself, and could result in you not being able to generate the results that you desire. Focusing on mastering just a few places first is a great opportunity to get your name out there, develop consistency, master the various aspects of the platform you are on, and build your brand. If you desire to expand after you always can, but just a few platforms are plenty early on.

## Outline Your Path

Once you have determined which platforms you are going to be on, you need to determine what your path is going to be for those platforms. In other words, you want to determine how you are going to be able to incorporate each of these platforms into your overall approach so that you can generate an entire brand image and message. If you look at other brands online, you will discover that each brand is using their different platforms with a slightly different approach to targeting their audience. This is because each platform has different uses, so they are leveraging the platforms in the way that works best for each platform itself in order to maximize their reach. As a result, they end up having different formats of content going out on each platform, but the general information contained within each piece of content is relatively the same from platform to platform. This way, their image remains consistent, yet dynamic, and they continue to reach a broader range of their audience. Furthermore, those who are following the brand on multiple platforms get different varieties of content as well so that they can stay up to date with their favorite brand without growing bored of the redundancy in information across all of the platforms.

Choosing how you want to outline your path for the platforms that you will be on starts with determining how you are going to get in front of your audience and what you are going to be sharing. Then, you need to discover how content is best shared on different platforms so that you can begin creating content specific to each platform. For example, Twitter responds best to short updates, so sharing brief updates about your brand on Twitter is a great opportunity to connect with your audience on Twitter. Then, you can elaborate that content for Instagram and place a nice image with the caption to ensure that it connects with your Instagram audience. Then, you can go live on Facebook about that content to share it, or share a status update around the same thing with your Facebook audience. Then, if you want to, you can download your Facebook live videos and upload them to YouTube so that you can begin connecting with your audience through YouTube. If you wanted to, you could even take it a step further and upload those YouTube videos to a blog on your website and into your emails as a newsletter that you share with your subscribers.

There are many ways that you can integrate the various platforms together to create a brand that rolls through and can easily be shared everywhere through all of the different strategies that work best on each platform. The more you learn how to cross-integrate these pieces of information, the easier it will be for you to create a larger online presence without having to create brand new content for every single platform. Even so, it is still best to start with a smaller number of profiles at first to avoid having to learn how to maximize your visibility on every platform at the same time. As you become more effective on each platform, you can start rolling into new platforms and developing your audience there. This way, you maximize your outreach and make it easier for you to grow your brand rapidly and fluidly.

You also want to consider how you are going to incorporate your offline branding strategies into your marketing plan, as these are just as important as online strategies for some brands. Finding ways to begin sharing with your audience offline and integrate those experiences into your online presence is a great opportunity for you to leverage multiple platforms at once. For example, perhaps you plan on going to networking events once a month in order to meet new people and collaborate on new projects or get connected with new clients. As you do, you can always connect with the people you meet online to broaden your online presence and increase your brand recognition on a local front. You can also start photographing yourself at these events and sharing them to your social media platforms with hashtags so that other people who are interested in local networking events find you online as well. This way, you not only build your brand dynamic but you also show people that you exist in the offline space. As a result, people who are local will know that you are creating a powerful local presence and will start to interact with you more as an effort to connect with you and your business. This will allow you to nourish your connections both online and offline so that you can continue growing your brand image and creating success for yourself. As a result, you will open up far more opportunities, leverage all of your person experiences, and enable your brand to grow far more rapidly than if you were to attempt to grow your online and offline presences separately.

# Chapter 6: Building Your Platform

The next step in building your personal brand is building your platform. Your platform is the space from where you will share everything for your brand so that your target audience can find you and begin working together with you and your brand. You want to focus on building your platform in a way that allows you to have a solid foundation that quickly and easily portrays your brand image as soon as people land on your platform. Then, as they scroll through the content that you compile for your brand in these profiles, they should see a very clear consistency in your image and content that helps them get clear on what your brand is all about and whether or not they resonate with what you are sharing. If your brand does not immediately convey what they need to know, chances are they will click away from you and start looking elsewhere to find someone who can do the same work that you can but who presented themselves in a better way.

## Learn How to Brand Your Platforms

First, you need to learn how to brand the platforms that you have chosen to be on when it comes to the online space. Learning how to customize your profiles so that you can create quick brand recognition is important, as you know, so you need to focus on creating this across every platform that you are going to be spending time on. Since there are so many different configurations that can be made on each platform, I have created a guide of what is important to integrate across all platforms, as well as some platform-specific information for all of the major platforms.

## For All Platforms

Each platform that you are on needs to have a similar aesthetic going on compared to your other profiles to ensure that people can easily recognize you across various platforms. This means that your profile pictures, profile header images, and any images that you share on your actual profile itself all need to have a similar aesthetic. They should share similar colors, elements, and qualities to make it look as though they are all thoughtfully designed to go together in a way that clearly expresses your brand to your audience.

In addition to your graphics being similar, you also want to use the same username across all profiles to ensure that people can easily find you anywhere online. Having different usernames everywhere can make it confusing for people to find you as they struggle to locate where you are online, which can make it challenging for you to grow your audience across multiple platforms. Rather than having your existing audience easily locate you elsewhere, you will have to rebuild from scratch on every single platform, which is ineffective at best.

Finally, make sure that your bio and any other written content you share on the platform is similar, too. You want to make sure that the language you use is similar across all platforms so that your audience gets the same message from you everywhere. This is going to ensure that you come across as authentic and consistent online, allowing you to continue attracting the same target audience everywhere and contributing content to support that target audience across all of your platforms.

## Instagram

Instagram is a photo-based sharing platform that thrives on

sharing visual content for your audience to see. That being said, captions are still a part of your Instagram experience so you do have the opportunity to include written content on your platform and have it read by your audience each time you share. You will want to be leveraging these as well as your stories, IGTV (video streaming) and live video streaming platforms on Instagram to make the most out of the platform and get the furthest reach.

Here is how you can brand your Instagram profile completely:

- Use a recognizable username
- Create a recognizable bio
- Use a recognizable profile photograph
- Upload your branded link
- Upload images that match your mood board and color scheme
- Write captions that are relevant to your target audience and your brand message
- Use hashtags that are relevant to your target audience; create your own branded hashtags
- Share branded stories; share behind the scenes of your brand
- Upload or live stream branded video content

## Facebook

Facebook business pages are a great platform for you to create a Facebook "profile" for your brand. Your page can do virtually everything a profile can do, except it is separate from your personal profile and people can freely follow it. On your page, you can upload live videos or prerecorded videos, share status updates, pictures, links, and even run polls.

Here is how you can brand your Facebook business page completely:

- Use a page name that is relevant to your personal brand, even if it is just your name
- Create a branded page username
- Use a branded profile picture and header image
- Upload your branded link
- Create an "About Me" section that explains your purpose and message
- Upload your branded services to a services tab
- Share content that is on brand
- Upload stories that are on brand

## Twitter

Twitter is a conversation-based platform where conversations are shared on large threads about topics that are trending from day to day. The biggest benefit of Twitter is that you can engage in conversations directly with your target audience and begin learning about exactly what they are interested in. Twitter gives you a great space to stay up to date on the trends in your industry so that you can stay relevant across all platforms and have an intimate understanding of how these trends are impacting your audience online. This way, you can stay ahead of the curve and leverage your knowledge to stay relevant across all platforms online.

Here is how you can brand your Twitter business profile completely:

- Use a recognizable username
- Use a branded profile picture
- Upload a branded header image
- Share a branded bio
- Upload your branded link
- Share branded content

## YouTube

YouTube is a platform were you can share video content directly with your audience. On other platforms, videos that are ten minutes or less tend to gain more traction — but on YouTube, your channel can thrive with longer episodes of content for your audience to watch. In fact, many channels find that their longer content produces better feedback than their shorter content because people generally enjoy watching longer videos on YouTube in general.

Here is how you can brand your YouTube channel completely:

- Branded channel name
- Branded profile picture
- Branded header image
- Branded video titles
- Branded video cover images
- Branded video content and themes
- Personalized "About Me" section
- Branded channel trailer

## LinkedIn

LinkedIn is the leading B2B social media platform online right now. LinkedIn works similarly to Facebook, though it has the opportunity to include a list of your skills and endorsements as it is meant to be used as your channel to share your professional brand with other professionals. LinkedIn allows you to connect directly with other professionals to either collaborate on projects or be hired as a service provider for them or their company.

Here is how you can brand your LinkedIn profile completely:
- Use your real name
- Include your professional title
- Upload your skills and ask for industry-specific endorsements
- Include your professional experience, both paid and voluntary
- Upload a branded profile picture
- Upload a branded header image

- Create a branded bio that explains who you are, what you do, and what your mission is
- Upload branded content

As long as you properly brand each platform, it will be easy for you to create a consistent image online for you to be discovered with. This will help people immediately know who you are, determine whether or not they are a part of your target audience, and decide whether or not they are going to follow you right from the start.

## Create High-Quality Graphics for All Platforms

Creating high quality graphics for your platforms does not have to be a challenging or expensive task. In fact, you can easily create high quality graphics for yourself using your branded colors and images on a platform like Canva or Photoshop so that you have high quality, customized graphics for all of your social media platforms. This way, everything you place on your page is intentional, branded, and unique to your brand.

Since you are just starting out, you might consider making yourself a brand kit. This is a kit that graphic designers will often make for businesses who want to keep their social media content relevant and consistent. A branding kit often contains header images for all of the social media platforms, plus backgrounds for quote images that you can create for your platform so that everything you share has a similar image.

You can also create presets on your phone, either on the social media platforms themselves or in a photo editor like Lightroom CC or VSCO so that you can use the same filters over and over again. This way, every image you share has a similar filter over it and therefore has similar colors to all of the other ones. These types of filter presets can either be custom created by yourself, or you can Google a tutorial for how you can create custom presets to help all of your images maintain a similar appearance.

It is important that all of your quote images, filters, and presets are similar across all of your social media platforms so that everything comes together nicely with your brand. Although you will need to make different dimensions for your pictures — and you may need to shift your elements to keep your profiles looking equally attractive — keeping similar elements, colors, and designs across all profiles is important. This will ensure that your brand has a consistent image everywhere, thus increasing brand recognition for your platform.

## Create High-Quality Written Content for All Platforms

In addition to graphics, you also need to be creating high quality written content across all of the platforms to ensure that you are remaining consistent in the quality of content and value that you are offering to people online. The written content you offer does not necessarily need to be lengthy, but creating content that contains high quality pieces of information and knowledge is a great opportunity to show your audience how much you know, position yourself as the expert, and start building relationships. When people see you posting content that they are interested in, they begin engaging with that content and wanting to get to know you more so that they can either learn more from you or collaborate more with you to create more great content. Both of these can be great opportunities in personal branding to keep you in the position of being able to leverage your brand effectively.

Creating high-quality content for each platform will vary slightly, as what may create great traction on one platform may not necessarily be ideal for others. Finding what type of content works on each platform is an important way to ensure that you are going to be able to create high-quality content for each platform, which will keep your platforms growing consistently. The easiest way to quickly identify what type of content works and what does not work is to look at other people in your industry on that platform and see what they are doing. Pay attention to how their content is unique, how they structure it, and what they are doing to get it in front of their audience to keep themselves visible and relevant. This is a great way to see how your industry behaves on each platform so that you can begin creating content similar to how other people are creating their content, which will allow you to begin creating high quality and targeted content right off the bat.

It is important that you do not completely copy other peoples' content when you look to theirs for inspiration, but rather get a feel for what works and allow that to inspire you to create success in your own posts. Ideally, you want to look at how they are wording things, what they are talking about, and how they are encouraging engagement with their audience in each post. You can also pay attention to what they are doing to generate sales through their content if you are looking to market so that you can get a feel for what works and what does not work.

In addition to looking at the people who are succeeding, look at the people who are not doing so well online and see what they may be doing wrong. Make sure that you are not looking at accounts that are newer, as these are likely people who are just starting out so they have yet to really maximize their momentum and grow rapidly. However, pay attention to the accounts of people in your industry who have been at it for a while and who have never gained momentum at all. See what these people are doing, and notice if there are any trends that are opposed to the trends of those who are actually succeeding. Sometimes, the trend is something obvious and other times it can be as simple as not having authentic or genuine content so their writing comes across as being uninteresting or fake in how it sounds. You want to avoid making the same mistakes that these people make so that you do not fail to gain momentum early on. The more momentum that you can create, the better your momentum will be and the further you will get with personal branding and leveraging your personal brand for opportunities.

When you are writing, make sure that you look at other factors that contribute to the quality of writing, too. Be sure to use a broad vocabulary, use words that resonate with your audience, and ensure that your writing is free of grammar, spelling, and punctuation errors. Keeping your content easy to read, high quality, and engaging is an important part of producing high quality written content for your audience to read.

## Find A Way to Share Similar Content

When it comes to growing your platform, it is important that your content tells a story and helps people grow with you. You also want to find a way to share similar content across all of your platforms so that all of your platforms come together to tell the same story, as this is a great way to really lock in consistency and create growth in your online platforms quickly. By creating stories on your online platforms that build on themselves and that weave together throughout your various platforms, you not only create consistency but you also create a brand that is easy to follow and understand as everything you are posting comes together in a powerful way.

As people follow you from day to day, everything you share makes sense because you are elaborating on previous content. Of course, you need to make sure that you do this in a way that allows you to appeal to new followers as well who may have missed out on previous content, so each piece of content will need to come together as an individual piece of a greater story.

Finding a way to share similar content can be easy, especially in a personal brand. One of the easiest ways to do it is to allow your information to flow through you and to share the building of information from day to day based on your actual life experiences. So, for example, say you are a life coach, you may invite your followers along on a journey to show them how you face struggle, what you do to manage hardships, and why you are qualified to help them with their own challenges. This type of process allows you to walk people through a story with you, build your brand for them, and keep them interested in you personally. Plus, because you are sharing personal stories, you are allowing your audience to have the opportunity to feel like they personally relate to you which keeps them feeling a strong relationship with your audience.

If you do not feel like sharing content as it comes up for you is doable, or if you feel like it is too awkward or uncomfortable to bring people along on your day-to-day life like that, you might consider creating monthly storyboards. These are essentially content calendars that allow you to put together an idea of how you want your content to flow over the course of a month so that you already know what to post about, allowing you to simply check your calendar and post. For some people, this can be easier than trying to come up with content on the spot which makes it easier to stay on task and consistent with the amount of content that you upload. It can also be helpful for people who like to schedule their content out on scheduler applications like Buffer or Hootsuite so that they can simply let the content automatically be uploaded each day.

## Practice Recycling Content

Recycling content is a common thing that many online brands will do to help leverage content that performed well in the past. Recycling content can happen in two ways: recycling content by slightly altering it for a different platform, or recycling content by saving popular posts and recreating them at a later date on the same platform. Either way, recycling content can be a great way to get your best performing content out there over and over again, so that existing followers can recall the information and new followers can receive it for the first time. That, or, followers on all platforms can receive the same great message in a way that is unique and helpful to that platform. Below you can find advice on how to effectively recycle content in both ways so that you can reuse great content without being seen as repetitive or redundant.

## Recycling Content for Different Platforms

Recycling content for different platforms can be quite simple, as all you need to do is either shorten or elongate the content to share again elsewhere. You may also benefit from sharing that content in a way that allows it to be received better based on the platform that you are speaking on to ensure that your audience actually receives it well. For example, if your audience on one platform tends to be more interested in feeling inspired in a playful way and your audience on another platform wants to be inspired in a more thought-provoking way, you can always adjust your content to be more focused on what your audience needs.

When you recycle content for different platforms, it is always a good idea to make sure that you adjust it a little bit even if it is two platforms where you can generally share in the same way so that your multi-platform followers can read your content in a new way. However, this is not necessary. You can certainly copy and paste content from one platform to another so they are up at the same time, or even do it a couple of days apart so that the content circulates longer. It is entirely up to you to decide how you are going to recycle the content, so long as you do it in a way that your audience is receptive to. Ultimately, you can choose whatever feels right and easiest for you so that you and your audience can both receive the benefits of the great content that you have already written and shared.

## Recycling Content for Later Use

Many personal brands recycle content for later use if the lesson in the content was high value. This is a great way to help information recirculate or to get it in front of your newer audience — however, it does need to be done properly to avoid being seen as redundant or annoying in the online space. If you recycle content too often, or too close together, people may think that you have nothing genuine or authentic to say and then they stop following you. It is typically a good rule of thumb to only share recycled content every so often so that you can share authentic content frequently, too, thus giving all of your followers plenty of great content to consume.

If you do want to recycle content, however, ensuring that you share content a few weeks apart at least will keep you from sharing the content too close together and having your audience feel annoyed at your recycled content. Ideally, sharing every 3-4 months or even longer is ideal to avoid having them too close together. You can always adjust the content slightly too so that the information is conveyed in a slightly new manner, thus giving the feeling of the content being brand new, even if it is not.

# Chapter 7: From Personal Brand to Profitable Brand

The final part of leveraging your personal brand is learning how to actually make a profit from your brand! Creating a personal brand is only worthwhile if you are going to be sharing in a way that allows you to actually generate a profit. Many people think that generating a profit from your personal brand requires you to only put yourself out there, and from that, you will automatically start getting new opportunities and offers from people in your industry. While this is part of it, it is also important that you make yourself known as being available to reach out to and to collaborate or work with so that people realize that you are actually seeking opportunities. The strategy of switching from being just a personal brand to a profitable one is rather simple, although it can take some practice if you are not used to marketing yourself.

In this chapter, you are going to discover how you can begin leveraging your personal brand to directly bring in opportunities and sales for you — thus making your personal brand profitable. You are going to do this by first identifying what skills you have that you can profit from, then turning those skills into a product or service, and lastly selling those skills so that you can make money. This chapter will be described in terms that reference the work that an entrepreneur or sole proprietor may do, but you can easily adapt these skills to create a personal brand that suits you. The way that personal branding works in both the corporate and entrepreneurial world is similar, so you can always adapt the information to serve either need.

## Find Your Sellable Features

First, you need to find what your sellable features are, or what you are particularly good at. In chapter 3, you identified what differentiated you from others — and at that point, you considered what your strengths were. It is important that you reconsider these strengths and look into them to identify what your unique skill set is and how you may be able to profit from that skill set so that people can begin to hire you or purchase from you. If you find that the strengths that you identified previously were not detailed enough, you can always begin looking for a way to identify your strong *skills* instead — either by reflecting on yourself or by asking those around you for their opinion.

Once you have found what skills you are great at, you can start identifying how they fit into your brand and how you can turn them into a product or a service that you can offer for sale. If you are not entirely sure as to what this might look like, you can always look around at others in your industry and see how they are selling their services. You may find that it is easier to create packaged deals and offer consulting or coaching services with your skills, or you may find it to be easier to put together pre-recorded videos and sell digital downloads of your content online. You may even find it to be easier to offer actual products, such as design packages or customized products created specifically for your customer. What you discover will depend on your industry, so stay open and get inspired for how your work may be able to come through. Once you find the way that fits your skillset, what you are interested in offering, and your target audience, you will find that it is easier for you to create a plan for how you can begin profiting off of your personal brand.

It is worth noting that if you have multiple skills that are relevant to your brand, creating multiple offers that will cater to various clients can be a great idea. Do not be afraid to identify all of your sellable skills that relate to your industry and then find ways to group them together so that you can turn them into profits later, in the next stage of turning your personal brand into a profitable brand. Catering to many different individuals in your audience through different brands is a great opportunity to increase your profitability and make even more money through your personal brand.

## Create Products or Services

Once you have identified what is trending in your industry and you have found a few ideas for what types of products and/or services you can create for your audience, you can begin conceptualizing products or services for you to begin offering yourself. Early on, the products or services that you offer may be fairly simple and even low cost entry to help you start building momentum in your business. Launching small services or very straightforward services like this can be a great opportunity for you to begin creating momentum in your business by connecting with paying clients, growing more confident in the services that you are offering, and generating testimonials. As your customer base grows, you will find that it becomes easier for you to begin creating larger or more complex services that also come at a higher price to support you in expanding your business and earning a higher income from it.

In the meantime, you want to focus on creating a high quality entry-level service or product that you can begin marketing and selling. Ideally, you want to create just one at first so that you can become highly familiar with that product or service, learn how to market it effectively, and feel confident in providing it to your audience. Doing this is not only going to help you in generating momentum and getting your offers out there, but it is also going to build your confidence in marketing yourself, sharing your products and services, and understanding how you can directly serve your audience in the best way possible. As you come to understand how your relationship with your clients works you will find it becomes easier for you to assert what value your clients will gain from you, thus making it even easier for you to sell and share more with your audience. Additionally, you will have the opportunity to listen to your clients and what they desire more or pay attention to any trends that they seem to have, which will make it even easier for you to determine what your next product or service should be for your audience.

# Learn the Art of Online Marketing

Once you have created your product or service that you want to offer to your audience, you can begin marketing your product. Marketing yourself in person should be fairly simple, you will just talk about what you have to offer and answer any questions as they arise naturally. As a result, people come to know who you are and what you have to offer and, if you offer what they are looking for, they will either hire you or take down your information so that they can contact you at a later date to discuss working together. Online, marketing is slightly different as it does take more work to start conversations and begin developing a connection and trust with your audience so that you can actually start making sales.

How you market online will depend on who your audience is and where they are spending their time online, but often the best way to begin marketing is to begin by talking about the product or service that you have to offer. Begin by sharing with people what it will be like for people to join you, what they can expect to gain from you, and how you can support them with getting their needs met through you. You can talk about the various elements of your service that will support them, the way that the service is offered, and why you are so passionate about the service that you are offering. The more you talk about the service that you are offering, the easier it becomes for you to be known for having that service available so people begin to recall you as being the go-to person to have that service fulfilled.

In addition to talking about your products or services and the many ways that they can benefit your audience, you can also show them. When it comes to products, showing your audience the value of your products often works by actually giving a demonstration through a video that shows how your products work, what they do, and why they are so unique and awesome. You can also do this for services, however, either by going live and showing off parts of the services that you offer, doing a live demonstration of the service if you can, or otherwise sharing as much as you can so that your audience begins to see your service.

In addition to emphasizing specifically on your services, you can also focus on giving your audience free content and support so that they start to get a feel for what it is like to work with you and how your knowledge can support them. For example, if your positioning yourself as a marketing expert and you offer consulting services, you can always share free content by giving off information about how to identify your target audience, how to make high quality graphics, or how to create sales funnels. Giving small pieces of valuable information with great tips can support your audience in understanding where your zone of genius lies so that they know what they need to be hiring you for.

## Start Asking for Sales

One of the key things that people forget about when it comes to converting their audience from followers to paying clients is the importance of asking for sales. Many people also try to overlook or avoid this step because it can be uncomfortable or awkward to ask for people to invest in you, especially if you are new in personal branding and are not entirely confident with your personal brand and offers, yet. Trust that the more you practice asking for sales, the more comfortable it will become which will actually increase the numbers of conversions that you begin receiving as a result of asking for the sale.

Asking for the sale can be simple, all you have to do is ask someone if they are interested in investing in your products or services. We often make this part of the process harder than it needs to be by feeling as though your audience should automatically know that the product or service is available, therefore they should be clear in the fact that you are available to actually offer it. That being said, many people find it easier to invest in someone when they are directly asked to, as they may feel uncomfortable asking themselves. Offering your product or service directly to people in conversations when you have been talking about your offers already is a great opportunity to help people realize that the offer does not merely exist, but it exists *for them.* As a result, they are more likely to invest in you and your offer so that they can receive your services and, in turn, you receive a new client who pays you and offers you the opportunity to receive a testimonial so that you can grow your momentum.

If you are uncomfortable with asking for sales, it can be helpful to start practicing and reflecting on where you were successful and where you were not successful in the process. This way, you can get a better idea of how you can generate greater success with your personal brand in the future when it comes to offering your services and asking for sales. Eventually, you will find a way to offer it that feels natural and that easily highlights the values of your products or services so that people are more likely to buy. As it starts to feel more natural and comfortable for you, it will also help it feel more natural and comfortable for your audience or the person that you are asking which will increase the likelihood of you receiving the sale.

One big reason why people never ask for the sale is that they are afraid of rejection or, worse, being ridiculed for offering something that the other person may not see as being a necessary product or service. Being afraid of offering your services is natural, and being afraid of receiving rejection or harsh feedback for offering your services is also natural. In our society, bullying is a very common thing and we are not often taught about how we can effectively handle the feelings that come with being rejected. Learning how to adjust your mindset so that you can begin feeling more confident that rejection is not a negative thing and that being ridiculed is a very uncommon thing can help you feel more confident in overcoming this fear. You will also find that as you get rejected more and more, your feelings of rejection are no longer as intense because you discover that being rejected is truly not that bad. When your product or service has been rejected, realize that it is not *you* being rejected, instead it is your audience rejecting the offer that you have made. This might happen because your offer is not aligned with that person at that moment, because they have not yet developed enough trust in you and your gifts, or because they are not presently in need of the services that you are offering. In some cases, consistent rejection may mean that your service needs to be adjusted or altered to help you begin creating more traction, as you may simply have a certain element of your service not jiving well with your audience.

## Collect Referrals

Finally, a huge opportunity to begin selling more of your products and services to your target audience lies in generating and collecting social proof around the value of your products, what you have to offer. Social proof is one of the most valuable marketing tools that you can use as it shows your audience that people have already invested in you and that they thoroughly enjoyed the products or services that they received. We have seen social proof be leveraged as a valuable tool throughout the ages — starting with when a business first comes to fruition and word of mouth was used to spread information about a business and support that business in receiving more traction from its target audience. We see it nowadays through testimonials and recommendations, and it has even grown to the point where an entire industry rose for the very purpose of leveraging social proof: the influencer industry. In this industry, every person in the industry has become well-known for establishing a large network of people who trust them and then marketing products or services to that audience so that they can earn a commission each time a product or service is sold.

Collecting referrals is a great opportunity to begin establishing social proof for your personal brand so that people can see how good you are at what you do. In order to be able to collect referrals, you need to be willing to ask your customers to actually give you one, which can be uncomfortable at times, particularly if you are not sure how you can ask for referrals. Typically speaking, the easiest way to ask for your clients to give you referrals is to straight out ask them and receive their answer of either yes or no. That being said, if that feels uncomfortable for you, you can also include a word about referrals in your follow-up information. For example, if you send out an automated "Thank You" email for your clients to receive the following working with you, you can ask for a referral in there. This way, you are always asking for referrals and have the opportunity to receive referrals from your audience.

Another great way to increase the quality of your referrals is to recommend that they are done in a couple of different ways. Your audience could easily go to your Facebook page or website and leave a review, or they could write you back in an email with one that you can easily use on your website or elsewhere. They could even leave you a video review so that you can share that with your audience. Giving your clients a variety of different ways that they can leave a review is a great opportunity for you to open them up to the idea of giving you referrals so that you can begin leveraging those referrals for social proof.

Once you start receiving referrals, you can leverage those referrals by sharing them around on the internet. You can start by sharing pictures of them in your stories or copy and pasting them into your status updates, and you can even turn them into testimonials for your website if you want to. The more you work toward sharing these referrals, the more people are going to see the positive feedback that you are getting from your paying clients, thus increasing their interest in working with you, too. As well, the more you share this information the more people may begin to recognize those who are leaving you with reviews so that you can begin to feel personally connected to you through a mutual contact, further increasing their trust in you.

# Section 3: Scaling Your Personal Brand

# Chapter 8: Taking Your Brand to the Next Level

Once you have built your brand and started generating momentum, you are going to need to start taking your brand to the next level so that you can really utilize your momentum. People who do not act on their momentum often find themselves quickly losing traction and struggling to scale their personal brands, which can result in all of your hard efforts being lost. The more you run with the momentum you have created for yourself, the more you will be able to scale your business. Scaling your business means not only earning more income but also increasing your credibility, perceived value, and chances of receiving aligned opportunities that can help you propel your momentum forward even further.

In this chapter, you are going to learn how to take the personal brand you have built and run with the momentum so that you can grow your business to new heights and truly thrive. You will notice that most of this chapter is focused on scaling practices that you have already been using so that you can start getting seen by a broader audience. That is because scaling a business is similar to establishing one and generating your initial audience — you simply need to remain devoted and continue building with the momentum. Some of your strategies will naturally shift over time, both because you will need more efficient ways of doing things as you grow and because you will begin to find more of what works for you. Still, the fundamentals of what it takes to establish your brand and scale your brand are similar.

## Extending Your Reach

First, you want to focus on extending your reach out even further than you already are so that you can begin drawing in new audience members. A great way to do this is through giveaways, advertisements, or opt-ins that can support you in providing new followers with a clear understanding of who you are and what you have to offer them. You can also extend your reach by encouraging your audience to share your content so that their audience can see it, too, making it more likely for you to be discovered by your target audience. Below are some great examples on how you can leverage these four practices to help you extend your reach.

## Giveaways

Giveaways are a great opportunity to extend your reach because you can leverage a giveaway to help get more people following you and your brand. Many online giveaways are entered by having your followers tag friends who they think would be interested in the giveaway, or by sharing your post on their profile so that their followers can see you. Since you are the one giving away things for free, you can decide what it takes for your audience to enter in the giveaway that you are offering. That being said, make sure that you pay attention to what each platforms' guidelines are to refrain from being banned from a platform for hosting a giveaway that goes against the guidelines of said platform.

Giveaways can be extremely simple, all you need to do is pick a product or service that you want to giveaway and then offer that product or service for free in exchange for people entering your giveaway. All giveaways have different ways of being entered, though some standard requirements for entrance include having to tag a friend, share the post, share a memory or a piece of information relating to the giveaway, or even submit your email at a certain link. These are all great ways to extend your reach and increase your ability to connect with your target audience so that you can scale your brand rapidly.

## Advertisements

Online, paid advertisements can be a powerful opportunity to grow your brand by getting in front of your target audience. Paid advertisements work by allowing you to purchase your way into a better position in your audiences' newsfeed so that you can begin being seen by your target audience who you may not have reached as effectively through organic marketing. It is important that you take your time and learn how to advertise on each platform so that your advertisements have maximum exposure. If you do not share your content effectively, you might find yourself spending a lot of money on advertisements that do not perform well. Ideally, you should wait a while to get a feel for who your converting target audience is so that you can create your advertisements to target these individuals specifically.

## Opt-Ins

Opt-ins are a great tool to increase your audience as they give you something to offer in exchange for someone's email address. As a result, you have direct access to a tool that you can use to connect with them on a regular basis and a way to help your audience find you online, too. Opt-ins are often small pieces of digital content or products that people can receive in exchange for their email address. There are many different types of opt-ins, each with different purposes. You will want to look around in your industry and get a feel for what types of opt-in offers are the most popular so that you can create a similar one and leverage it to get more leads.

## Encouraging Sharing

You can also increase your reach by encouraging your audience to share your content. Asking your audience to share a post that might resonate with their friends is a great opportunity for you to increase your reach by getting put in front of your audience's audience, which is likely to be filled with individuals who are also a part of your target audience. You can easily make your posts sharable by offering high-quality content and then requesting that your audience share the content with their friends and family if they think anyone might be interested. Including a word about sharing is a great way to remind your friends and family that they can share your content, which increases their likelihood of actually doing it.

## Increasing Your Engagement

In addition to getting in front of a broader range of people, you also want to increase the amount to which people are engaging with your existing content to ensure that your existing audience is actively building a strong relationship with you. This is also going to increase the popularity of your post, making it more visible due to the way that most social media platforms work. As a result, each piece of content that you share with your audience is going to be more valuable and create a larger impact, because more people are seeing it and responding.

You can increase engagement either by asking for it or perpetuating it. For example, sharing questions at the bottom of your posts that encourage people to answer in the comments is a great opportunity to increase your engagement on social media. You can also share content that inspires conversations by sharing your opinion and opening up the comment section for your audience to share their opinion, too, which creates an opportunity for them to engage with you. Another great way to encourage engagement is to share updates or memes that are highly likely to be shared and engaged with, as this makes it more likely that people will just naturally begin engaging.

Another great way to increase your engagement is to engage with others. Social media heavily revolves around social aspects, so it is important that you are being social as well to encourage people to want to socialize back with you. Asking people how they are doing, creating friendships and connections, and establishing relationships through comments and direct messages is a great opportunity to increase the number of relationships that you are building through your audience. As you engage with people, they start to become familiar with your name and with your brand, which results in them connecting with you even more.

## Creating Brand Loyalty

Another way that you can increase engagement is by creating brand loyalty. Remember: your audience engages with many people on a regular basis, they are also the same audience that many other people will be targeting. If you do not leverage your momentum and continue growing, you are going to find yourself rapidly declining in popularity as more people find their way to other people who are doing what you are doing. However, if you focus on creating brand loyalty, you can increase the likelihood of people continuing to follow your brand over other's so that you are more likely to make the sales and book the clients.

Creating brand loyalty comes through many ways, but ultimately it comes through respecting your audience and seeing them as valuable. Showing your audience that you believe them to be valuable is important, too, as it allows them to feel like you truly see them and care about them which results in your audience feeling special to you. You can help your audience feel special to you by sharing their content, having conversations with them, sharing their reviews in areas where they get "spotlighted" such as in your stories, or even by talking about their reviews yourself in your calls. You can also increase brand loyalty by offering incentives for people to follow your brand, such as special discounts or exclusive deals that no one else is getting. These types of strategies keep people paying attention because it helps them feel valued and gives them an incentive to stick around. The more you share with your audience, the more you are going to cultivate and deepen your relationship with your audience so that they experience a higher sense of brand loyalty and they are more likely to keep following you.

## Giving Them a Reason to Come Back

It is not enough to simply give your audience what they want and then allow them to move on. Simply put: meeting new loyal customers can be challenging, and your brand will heavily benefit from having your audience feel like they have a legitimate reason to come back or continue working with you. You can do this by having multiple offers available that cater to your audience, by creating new offers regularly, and by maintaining offers that are consumable so that people can continue purchasing them over and over again. The more you continue giving your audience more of what they are looking for, the more they will pay attention and continue coming back so that they can keep doing business with you. Plus, loyal followers and clients are always more likely to bring in even more loyal followers and clients, which can result in you creating massive success in your brand.

## Creating Higher-Value Offers

You may have noticed that one of the best ways to keep people coming back is to continue offering new things that they can purchase from you. You can also offer them consumable things that can be purchased regularly, such as products that run out, scheduled services, or memberships so that your audience has a reason to continue buying from you. As you grow and create new offers, focus on offering things that are higher in value so that your audience can keep purchasing from you and each offer begins to earn you more. That being said, you can also create lower cost offers so that those who cannot afford your higher-valued offers can purchase your lower priced offers and work with you anyway. This not only ensures that you reach as many people as possible but also results in those who purchased your lower cost offers seeing how it feels to work with you so that they can decide for themselves whether or not they want to get in on your higher-priced offers.

# Chapter 9: Taking Action!

Finally, you need to get started with taking action! You now have all of the information that you need to build your brand, generate an audience, and start scaling your brand — so now, you need to get started! Taking action with your brand can seem scary at first, but as you keep going, you will find that it gets easier and easier for you to take that action. The reality is: oftentimes, the fear that holds you back from *really* getting started and putting yourself out there is the fear of rejection or the fear of being found. In this chapter, we are going to discuss how you can feel confident getting your brand out there, taking action, and scaling your brand to greater heights so that you can leverage your brand for all of the benefits that we discussed in chapter 2.

## Getting Started

The first, and hardest thing for most people, is actually getting started. Often, there are two reasons why someone will refrain from getting started when it comes to personal branding: either they feel that more needs to be done before they can reasonably begin, or they feel that they are afraid of being rejected or ridiculed by their target audience. The reality is that both of these resistances are a frame of mind and not actual fact. You can always start where you are at, and people are a lot less mean than we often believe they will be, so you are unlikely to be negatively received by your target audience. In fact, most times people who put themselves out there are automatically received in a positive way and find that this continues to get better and better as they go.

If you find that you have been avoiding starting because you are afraid of what might happen or you feel like you are not ready yet, it is a good idea to start looking into your mindset. Ask yourself what you are so afraid of, why you believe you have to have it all together to start, and how you think you can show up best. Get clear on what you are actually afraid of, and then focus on building confidence in yourself and in your abilities so that you no longer feel so afraid of getting out there and in front of your audience. This is a great opportunity to start leveraging your mindset in a positive way so that you can set yourself up for success, rather than closing yourself off and finding yourself feeling unworthy or not good enough to start a new brand.

Many brands have started before they were ready, and many more have had plenty of negative feedback yet have had far more positive feedback that supported them in growing. In fact, Coca-Cola only sold 12 bottles in their first year in business, and now they are one of the largest soft beverage corporations in the western world. If you think that some rejection or resistance is enough to prevent success from happening, it may be ideal for you to begin researching brands who started out small or even those who struggled at first so that you can see how far they have come and so that you can allow yourself to realize that it truly is possible.

## Putting Your Brand Out There

Next, you really need to focus on putting your brand out there. It is not enough to speak about it one or two times then find yourself feeling rejected or put off when people do not immediately respond in a positive way to your marketing. You need to keep sharing, keep showing up, and keep getting your information out there so that people see that you are in business now and that you are not going anywhere any time soon. The more consistent you remain, the more credibility you will gain and therefore the more momentum you will develop. You want to continue developing on that momentum to keep yourself growing and moving forward.

If putting your brand out there feels scary and uncomfortable, you may want to look into yourself and see how you can develop your confidence more. Since your brand is rooted in who you are and in what you have to offer, it can be easy to let a lack of self-confidence or a lack of self-esteem prevent you from growing. However, if you notice this behavior as it starts then begin clearing it out as soon as possible. If you work at growing your confidence by stepping beyond your comfort zone on a regular basis, is soon becomes easier. If you find that you are feeling particularly out of place because of sharing with people who are not also sharing, you might consider surrounding yourself with other people who are branding themselves online, too. Sometimes, being surrounded by your peers and competition online can help you feel more confident in putting yourself out there because you are witnessing so many others doing the same thing.

## The Early Stages of Getting Found

At first, it can be challenging to remain faithful in your

business if you feel like you are not gaining traction because no one seems to be engaging with you or purchasing from you. It is normal for businesses to take some time to gain traction so do not be afraid of your business not growing as fast as you would like if it does not take off immediately. Instead, continue sharing and building confidence in yourself and everything that you have to offer, and practice marketing your content. Once you begin getting clients, you can start leveraging that and their referrals as an opportunity to book even more clients. Before you know it, you will be booking clients effortlessly, maximizing your momentum in your business, and generating success online. The beginning is nearly always the hardest part.

If you feel that you are truly not getting found at all and that you are having a terribly hard time building any base level of momentum, you may benefit from looking through your marketing strategies and adjusting to becoming more authentic and impactful with your marketing materials. As you do, your content will start to flow better and you will likely find that you gain far more traction through your online engagements and efforts.

Finally, if you really feel like you are struggling to gain

traction, you may need to do more work around building relationships with people. Do not be afraid to reach out to your followers and people who you admire and start conversations, as this is a great opportunity for you to begin learning more about the people in your industry. Through this, you also build relationships which could eventually become great tools for you to increase your bookings. In fact, some of your new relationships may even become clients, making this a super valuable tool. When reaching out to people, seek to generate positive and engaging relationships that nurture connection so that these individuals begin to trust and respect you. If you begin starting relationships just to generate more sales, people are going to see you as phony or pushy and may resist working with you for fear of being trapped into a pushy relationship.

## Making Yourself Available for Opportunities

In addition to getting yourself out there, you also need to make sure that you are available to be approached. There is nothing worse than having yourself advertised as being available for opportunities and then having no time or desire to actually take anyone up on the opportunities that they are offering you. Make sure that you clear space in your calendar and become available for the right opportunities, and then make sure that you treat each opportunity with respect by holding up your end of the bargain. The more you become available for opportunities and treat those opportunities respectfully, the better your momentum will evolve and the easier it will be for you to book more clients.

Beyond making yourself available on the calendar, make sure that you also communicate that you are available in your marketing materials so that anyone who may be considering offering you an opportunity knows that you are actually available to take them up on that offer. If you come across as closed off or uncertain about where you stand, people are going to think that you are closed off or uncertain and they are going to refrain from offering you any opportunities. Even if you seem like a good fit, most people do not want to invade someone's privacy and will refrain from offering altogether rather than pushing themselves in front of you. So, if you want opportunities, be open and inviting and make sure that people know you are available to take on these opportunities.

# Finding Your First Clients

Finally, you want to get yourself out there by finding your first clients. If you do everything that you have been shown in this book, particularly when it comes to building and scaling platforms, getting clients should be fairly simple. Still, you may find that getting your first few clients takes a little more effort as you have yet to establish a name for yourself. If this is the case, there are a few things that you can consider doing to help kick start your brand and book clients.

First, you can reach out to your family and friends and let them know that you are officially in business and offering services and you can ask them to consider referring their friends and family your way if they would fit with your services. Asking for referrals from people who already know you is excellent because these are individuals who personally know you — therefore, they can personally recommend you, and their word means more.

Another thing you can try is offering your audience discounts, deals, or even doing a small amount of pro bono work to get your audience to do some work with you. Once they have, you can ask them for a referral and use these referrals to begin generating a larger buzz around you and your brand so that your larger offers have more traction. Then, as you start generating these referrals, you can begin charging full price and leveraging that momentum to grow even more. This way, you can start booking plenty of clients to keep your personal brand afloat.

If you have asked for support and find that you continue to struggle to get clients, it may be valuable to look at what you are offering and how you are leveraging your platform. You may find that your offers are not aligned with your audience or that your platform is confusing or unclear, which can result in you not being able to effectively communicate with and book new clients. Adjusting this can support you in developing your personal brand and getting those first clients booked!

# Conclusion

This book was written to support you in launching your personal brand so that you can begin leveraging your skills and strengths to become self-sufficient in 2019. Launching a personal brand is not the easiest thing to do, but I hope that this book has provided you with plenty of information to help you feel like it is manageable. The more you work toward building your brand, leveraging your foundation, and scaling your platforms — the more you are going to be able to grow and succeed with your personal brand.

I hope that through reading this book, you now feel confident in understanding what it will take you to succeed and that you feel confident in yourself and in your ability to create a personal brand. Although there are certainly many elements of technical and professional aspects that need to be considered, there are also elements of authenticity and genuine connection that need to be considered. The more you share authentically and genuinely with your audience through the strategies offered to you from within this book, the more you are going to be able to leverage and scale your brand massively.

The next step after reading this book is to begin taking action and putting your brand out there. You may feel uncertain as to whether or not you are ready to take this step, but trust that the very fact that you are reading this brand proves that you are ready to begin taking action. Allow yourself to dive in and begin getting your name out in front of people so that you can begin establishing your credibility and authority. The more you share, the more you are going to be able to get seen in the online space — thus allowing you to create an even bigger name for yourself. Even if you feel completely out-of-place at first, share anyway and allow it to become practice as you begin to learn how to leverage your online platform and connect with your target audience.

Lastly, if you enjoyed reading this book and felt that it added value to your life and supported you in understanding how to establish a personal brand for yourself in 2019, please consider leaving a review. Your honest feedback would be greatly appreciated.

Thank you, and best of luck in building and scaling your personal brand!

www.ingramcontent.com/pod-product-compliance
Lightning Source LLC
Chambersburg PA
CBHW030702220526
45463CB00005B/1866